W9-AGJ-499

Illustrated by Paul Joy

The MIRACLE MORNING
ART of AFFIRMATIONS

A Positive Coloring Book for Adults and Kids

Hal Elrod • Brianna Greenspan

With Honorée Corder

GET THE MIRACLE MORNING APP!

Your Morning Routine Companion

The Miracle Morning app is a resource that supports you
in implementing everything you learn in the book.

Download the app at MiracleMorning.com/App

WATCH THE MOVIE FREE!

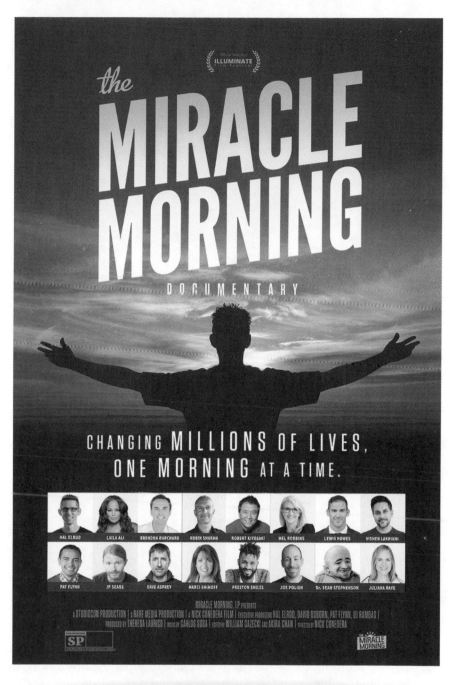

Changing Millions of Lives One Morning at a Time

Watch this life-changing film that brings the book to life and shows you how to join the millions of people who are transforming their lives, one morning at a time.

Watch now at MiracleMorning.com/Movie

THE MIRACLE MORNING: ART OF AFFIRMATIONS

Hal Elrod, Brianna Greenspan
with Honorée Corder

Copyright © 2022 by Hal Elrod International, Inc. All rights reserved.

Cover Copyright © 2022 by Hal Elrod International, Inc.

No part of this publication may be reproduced or transmitted in any form or by any means, mechanical or electronic, including photocopying and recording, or by any information storage and retrieval systems, without permission in writing from the author or publisher (except by a reviewer, who may quote brief passages and/or show brief video clips in a review).

Disclaimer: The advice and strategies contained herein may not be suitable for every situation. This work is sold with the understanding that the Author and Publisher are not engaged in rendering legal, accounting, or other professional services. Neither the Author nor the Publisher shall be liable for damages arising herefrom. The fact that an organization or website is referred to in this work as a citation or a potential source of further information does not mean that the Author or the Publisher endorses the information that the organization or website may provide or recommendations it may make. Further, readers should be aware that Internet websites listed in this work may have changed or disappeared between when this work was written and when it is read.

Cover Design: Matt Duncan, MattDuncan.co
Graphic Design: Paula Kelman, PaulaKelman.com
Illustrations: Paul Joy
Interior Design: Dino Marino, DinoMarino.com

Since I started doing positive affirmations, my life has been filled with an abundance of positivity and gratitude. It helps me focus on the things I desire in my life while remaining conscious of when negativity may be creeping in. This daily practice has not only created a new level of awareness around the thoughts and words I use myself but even better, it has had a direct impact on those around me that I love and care about. My daughter and wife do them with me, and together we get to appreciate all the blessings we have and desire as a family.

    – Matt Aitchison, Founder, Millionaire Mindcast

What a great idea! Since coloring has been shown to reduce stress and anxiety and spark creativity, coupling it with empowering messages makes so much sense. Plus the pages are fun and full of intricate designs. It had me grabbing for my coloring pencils instantly.

    – Amiee Mueller, Author, *Destination Awesome*

The Miracle Morning: Art of Affirmations is a fun way to bring a sense of play to your Life SAVERS routine and get creative while discovering affirmations that are meaningful to you. It's also an ideal way to introduce your kids to a powerful morning ritual that can have a positive impact on their day and their whole lives. It can be challenging to come up with an affirmation that feels authentic. Hal, Brianna and Paul have done a beautiful job of creating an engaging space for you to do just that. Enjoy!

    – Julianna Raye, Founder, Unified Mindfulness

As an entrepreneur in the social entrepreneur space it is easy to become discouraged as the challenges of operating your own small business stack up. Tools like this creative and empowering coloring book Hal, Brianna and Paul have developed will provide that much needed moment of re-centering when plans don't seem to be following your play book. As a parent I can't wait to share this with my teens who face similar challenges as they work to master the game of life. Thanks for this exceptional tool that's sure to be an instant best seller.

    – Dafna Michaelson Jenet, Author, *It Takes a Little Crazy to Make a Difference*

I coordinate C.H.A.R.M.S. at my school and it is wonderful to see my students begin to take the lead and take ownership of their mindset. My students take joy in setting their intentions and picking the activity of the day. They always look forward to Affirmations and Meditation. This book has changed how we start our day!

    – Natasha Letze, Fountain Elementary

— A SPECIAL INVITATION —

The Miracle Morning: Art of Affirmations Community

Thank you for choosing *The Miracle Morning: Art of Affirmations* (AOA) coloring book. We realize that there are hundreds of coloring books that you could have chosen, and we are thrilled that you decided to unleash your inner artist while simultaneously reinforcing positive affirmations!

Please use the AOA coloring book to inspire you, to relax you, to empower you, to ground you, to spark your imagination, and to get those creative juices flowing.

This coloring book has been designed to combine affirmations with mindful artistry. Visualize the success you are looking to create and use the affirmations within this book as inspiration along your journey. Choose affirmations that resonate with you. While creating your work of art, say the affirmation to yourself or out loud. Focus on visualizing that affirmation becoming a reality.

It's your coloring book, so personalize it in any way your heart desires. Use crayons, colored pencils, markers, paints, chalk ... there is no right or wrong way! Only your way!

Bonus Idea for Your Affirmations

Throughout the book, there are various pages that you can cut out to place your personalized Miracle Morning affirmations in highly visible areas of your life, such as your desk, bathroom mirror, nightstand, car, or any other place you spend time throughout your day.

Review and repeat your favorite affirmations over and over again to focus and program your mind for success. Be sure to share these creations with your friends and family and enlist their help in pursuing your new goals and commitments as well.

When you see your beautiful work of art, appreciate your own creativity and say the affirmation out loud or to yourself.

Join the movement today, and make *The Miracle Morning: Art of Affirmations* coloring book part of your everyday life! Unleash you inner artist by coloring your favorite quotes and affirmations, and share pictures of your finished creations in TMM Art of Affirmations Community (on Facebook) at **www.TMMAOACommunity.com**.

— DEDICATION —

Hal

This book is dedicated to the people who
mean more to me than anything in the world—my family.
Mom, Dad, my sister, Hayley, my wife, Ursula,
and our two children—Sophie and Halsten.
I love you all more than I can put into words!
This book is also in loving memory of my sister,
Amery Kristine Elrod.

Brianna

Keep Shining, The World Needs Your Light!

I dedicate this burst of positivity
to all who have loved, supported, and prayed for me.
Each and every one of you have made a profound impact
on my life. This book would not have been possible
without all the positive encouragement.

Paul

I dedicate the creativity
and positivity in this book
to my family and all those
who need a burst of color in their lives.

— CONTENTS —

— THE ART OF AFFIRMATIONS —

Welcome to *The Miracle Morning: Art of Affirmations*. As scientific studies have proven, the way we talk to ourselves is one of the greatest determining factors of our happiness, our health, and our success. Affirmations, *when done correctly*, are one of the most effective tools for programming your mind to become the person you need to be to achieve everything you want in your life.

Nonetheless, affirmations also get a bad rap. Many people have tried them, only to be disappointed, and see little or no results.

The reason for the disappointment is that the old way of doing affirmations is far from ideal, and can even be counter-productive. For decades, countless so-called experts and gurus have taught affirmations in ways that have proven to be ineffective and set you up for failure. There are two common problems with affirmations.

First, lying to yourself doesn't work.

I am a millionaire. Are you?

I have 7 percent body fat. Do you?

I have achieved all of my goals this year. Have you?

This method of creating affirmations that are written as if you've already become or achieved something may be the single biggest reason that affirmations haven't worked for most people.

With this technique, every time you recite an affirmation that isn't rooted in truth, your subconscious will resist it. As an intelligent human being who isn't delusional, lying to yourself repeatedly will never be the optimum strategy. The truth will always prevail.

The second problem with the way affirmations have been taught is that passive language doesn't produce results. Many affirmations have been designed to make you feel good by creating an empty promise of something you desire. For example, here is a popular money affirmation that's been perpetuated for decades by many world-famous gurus:

I am a money magnet. Money flows to me effortlessly and in abundance.

To generate financial abundance (or any result you desire, for that matter), you've got to actually *do* something. Your actions must be in alignment with your desired results, and your affirmations must articulate and affirm both.

When worded correctly, affirmations are designed to program both your conscious and subconscious mind to be in alignment with the focus and beliefs you need to move confidently toward your goals and dreams as well as reinforce the necessary behaviors that are required for you to make consistent progress.

The Miracle Morning: Art of Affirmations coloring book is designed to help you (and your family) to harness the power of affirmations in a way that is both fun and life-changing. Color them, cut them out, hang them on your vision board, frame them, or just leave them in the coloring book. It's totally up to you.

Either way, I'm excited for you to begin this new journey and hope that it will make you happier, healthier, and deepen your connection with the people you love.

With love,

Hal

— WHAT IS THE MIRACLE MORNING? —

What began as one person's desperate yet strategic attempt to take his life to the next level became a #1 best-selling book, and has now become a worldwide movement that has transformed hundreds of thousands of lives.

No matter where you are in your life right now, whether you are succeeding at the highest level, struggling to make it through each day, or somewhere in between, *The Miracle Morning* has proven to be the fastest way to take any area of your life to the next level, *even if you're not a morning person.*

What are the Life S.A.V.E.R.S.?

The Miracle Morning routine is made up of the six most powerful, effective, and time-tested personal development practices known to man … known as the Life S.A.V.E.R.S.

Robert Kiyosaki, #1 best-selling author of *Rich Dad Poor Dad*, said it best: "What Hal has done with his acronym S.A.V.E.R.S. is take the best practices—developed over centuries of human consciousness development—and condensed the 'best of the best' into a daily morning ritual. A ritual that is now part of my day.

Many people do *one* of the SAVERS daily. For example, many people do the *E*, they *exercise* every morning. Others do *S* for *silence* or meditation, or *S* for *scribing*, journaling every morning. But until Hal packaged SAVERS, no one was doing all six, ancient 'best practices' every morning.

The Miracle Morning is perfect for very busy, successful people. Going through SAVERS every morning is like pumping rocket fuel into my body, mind, and spirit … *before* I start my day, every day."

You can customize the Life S.A.V.E.R.S. to fit your lifestyle and use them daily to accelerate how quickly you're able to improve any area or achieve any results.

The Art of Repetition

Whether or not we realize it, incessantly talking to one's self is not just for crazy people. Every one of us has an internal dialogue that runs through our heads almost nonstop. Most of it is unconscious, that is, we don't consciously choose the dialogue. Instead, we allow our past experiences—both good and bad—to replay over and over again. Not only is this completely normal, it is one of the most important processes for each of us to learn about and master. Yet very few people take responsibility for actively choosing to think positive, proactive thoughts that will add value to their lives.

Your self-talk has a dramatic influence on your level of success in every aspect of your life—confidence, health, happiness, wealth, relationships, etc. Your affirmations are either working for or against you, depending on how you use them. If you don't consciously design and choose your affirmations, you are susceptible to repeating and reliving the fears, insecurities, and limitations of your past.

When you actively design and write out your affirmations to be in alignment with what you want to accomplish and who you need to be to accomplish it—and commit to repeating them daily (ideally *out loud*)—they immediately make an impression on your subconscious mind. Your affirmations go to work to transform the way you think and feel so you can overcome your limiting beliefs and behaviors and replace them with those you need to succeed.

You can use affirmations to start programming yourself to be confident and successful in everything you do simply by repeatedly telling yourself who you want to be, what you want to accomplish, and how you are going to accomplish it. With enough repetition, your subconscious mind will begin to believe what you tell it, act upon it, and eventually manifest it in your reality.

Putting your affirmations in writing makes it possible for you to choose your new programming, so it moves you toward that desired condition or state of mind by enabling you to consistently review it. Constant repetition of an affirmation will lead to acceptance by the mind. Since you get to choose and create your affirmations, you can design them to help you establish the thoughts, beliefs, and behaviors that you want and need to succeed.

The Art of a Vision Board

Vision boards were made popular by the best-selling book and film, *The Secret*. A vision board is simply a poster on which you place images of what you want to have, who you want to become, what you want to do, where you want to live, etc.

Creating a vision board is a fun activity you can do on your own, with a friend, your significant other, or even your kids. It gives you something tangible to focus on during your visualization. If you'd like detailed instructions on this process, Christine Kane has an excellent blog post, "How To Make A Vision Board," as well as a free eBook titled *The Complete Guide To Vision Boards*. Both are available on her website at www.ChristineKane.com.

Keep in mind that, although creating a vision board is fun, nothing in your life changes without action. I have to agree with Neil Farber, MD, PhD, who said in his article on psychologytoday.com, "Vision boards are for dreaming, action boards are for achieving." While looking at your vision board every day may increase your motivation and help you stay focused on your goals, know that only by taking the necessary actions will you get real-life results.

The Art of Mindfulness

Mindfulness is a style of meditation that is not religious in any way, so anyone can practice it. Research has shown amazing benefits from practicing mindfulness such as lower stress, lower blood pressure, stronger immune system, improved focus and productivity, greater creativity, better emotional regulation, and a better sleep cycle, to name a few! The system of Unified Mindfulness has been taught at many Miracle Morning events. Also, it has been used in breakthrough research at Harvard Medical School and taught at companies like Google and Green Mountain Coffee. In the system of Unified Mindfulness, *mindfulness* is defined as a set of three attention skills that work together: concentration power, sensory clarity, and equanimity. Some meditation styles hint at these skills. Unified Mindfulness likes to spell them out so there's no confusion and you make the most of your time practicing.

Concentration power is the ability to focus on what you choose. For example, getting deeply absorbed in the experience of repeating your affirmation! Sensory clarity is the ability to track your sensory experience in real time. For example, noticing subtle details as you repeat your affirmation! Equanimity is the ability to allow sensory experience to come and go without push and pull. For example, while repeating your affirmation, someone interrupts you and you become momentarily annoyed. Equanimity means you don't get caught in that feeling of annoyance, but you don't reject it either. You let it come and go as an experience inside you. On the flip side, let's say you're enjoying yourself so much as you repeat your affirmation, that you don't want the enjoyment to ever fade. Enjoyment comes and goes, so equanimity means letting that enjoyment get as big as it wants to and also being willing to let the experience of enjoyment go when it's time for it to be over. When you fight with your inner experience or when you try to hold on to it, you create little resistances that add up over time, dulling your experience of life overall.

The Art of Incorporating Mindfulness Into Your Coloring Practice

As you say your affirmation aloud or to yourself, make sure you also develop concentration, clarity, and equanimity. So for example, let's say your affirmation is "I'm making the world a more loving place." Concentration power means you really listen to yourself saying that phrase again and again. Each time your attention wanders away from it, you bring your attention back to hearing yourself say the phrase out loud or to yourself, "I'm making the world a more loving place." Sensory clarity means you notice subtle details as you say the phrase. For instance, you may notice how loud you're saying the phrase or with how much intensity. You may notice the consonants and vowels or changes in pitch as you say your affirmation. You may also notice the stops and starts as the phrase begins and ends or in between words. Another way to think about equanimity is that you become more interested in your present moment experience of saying your affirmation than you are concerned about future outcomes.

You improve the future by doing your best to bring concentration, clarity, and equanimity to your experience in this moment. If you're using emotions and visualization to enhance your affirmation, the same rules apply—concentrate on, become clear about, and bring acceptance to what you're seeing and feeling as you visualize and tap into your emotional life while doing your affirmation.

The Art of Meditation

Meditation is any practice that either implicitly or explicitly develops concentration power, sensory clarity, and equanimity. In order for meditation to have a powerful effect, it needs to develop those three skills.

The Art of Enhancing Your Coloring Experience by Turning It Into a Meditation

There are three basic categories that cover any experience we ever have: see, hear, and feel. *See* includes what you see in the mind, such as a visualization. It also includes what you see in the world. For example, the page with the affirmation you're choosing to color and the marker you're holding. *Hear* includes what you hear in the mind, such as an affirmation, and it also includes what you hear in your environment. For example, you might notice as you color that the room is pleasantly silent. *Feel* includes emotional sensations such as enjoyment or annoyance and also includes physical sensations, such as your breathing or the way a crayon or marker feels as you hold it in your hand. This category also encompasses taste and smell.

As you color, you can notice one aspect of your experience and keep your attention there for a few seconds. Then repeat that process again and again so the whole experience of coloring becomes a meditation. For example, first you might notice that you're seeing the affirmation on the page you're coloring. With a gentle matter-of-fact tone, you could say the label *see* to yourself or out loud and stay with what you're looking at for a few seconds. Then you might notice that the room is quiet. Again with a gentle, matter-of-fact tone, you could say the label *hear* to yourself or out loud and stay with noticing the quiet room for a few seconds. You can concentrate on the silence of the room or any other experience you notice at the same time as you continue to color.

Then, you might notice that you're feeling the marker in your hand. You would say the label *feel* to yourself and stay with that experience for a few seconds. Then you might notice you're feeling happy as you color. You would use that same label *feel* and stay with the experience of happiness for a few seconds. Staying with each different experience you notice for a few seconds and saying the label *see, hear* or *feel* in your mind depending on what you notice, helps develop concentration power, sensory clarity and equanimity. The labels keep you on track so you don't get lost in thought, which develops concentration power. The labels also get you into the habit of noticing what you're experiencing when and whether it's mainly *see, hear* or *feel*. That develops sensory clarity. Saying the labels in a gentle matter-of-fact way also help you have equanimity with whatever you're experiencing. Whether the experience is pleasant or unpleasant you're doing your best simply to notice it and appreciate it.

If you'd like to learn more about how to practice mindfulness, you can go to **UnifiedMindfulness.com/Core** for a free training.

What are the C.H.A.R.M.S.?

Do you know the feeling when you get out of bed and stretch and make the bed? That feeling is a sense of accomplishment. Your day already started out on a positive note. Students might not always come from a home that starts peacefully. Oftentimes, they are ripped from sleep by the blare of an alarm or parent's call. Then it is a mad dash to get dressed, get fed, collect bags, and rush to get to school. The student doesn't even have a chance to breathe!

C.H.A.R.M.S is a program that helps children pause, reflect, and start their day right. It utilizes S.A.V.E.R.S but with elementary schools and younger students in mind. C.H.A.R.M.S. is an acronym for Creativity, Health, Affirmation, Reading, Meditation, and Service.

Each day you focus **2-10 minutes** on one of the elements as you start your day.

By embracing The Morning Miracle and C.H.A.R.M.S/S.A.V.E.R.S you are providing a chance for the children and adults to catch their breath, set their intention, and activate their frontal lobes. The students will embrace a new growth mindset, strategies to self-soothe, and vocabulary to explain their needs. They will be following the example of leaders, musicians, thinkers, athletes, and more across the country!

How to use the Art of Affirmations

Feel free to use every affirmation as a journaling prompt. Ask yourself powerful questions. Perfect example, *I am ready and committed to make this my best year yet*. Ask yourself, what are you ready and committed to do to make this your best year yet?

As you journal on, visualize the answers to every single affirmation throughout this book, I invite you to start taking action that's in alignment with whatever comes up for you during your journaling

The Miracle Morning: Art of Affirmations empowers you to stay motivated, organized, and focused by strengthening your new positive habits and increasing your productivity.

Activities include:

Dreams Box - Use the miniature images to make a Dreams Box. You're welcome to decorate a box with affirmations and then write down your dreams and revisit them when you feel the need for a little bit of extra inspiration or share them with family, friends, or as community-wide activity.

Vision Board- Feel free to use the miniature images to add to your vision board so that affirmations can be part of your growth journey.

Gratitude Box - Use the miniature images to make a Gratitude Box. Write down one or multiple things you're grateful for each day and when the time is right, revisit them. This is a perfect family activity during breakfast that you can revisit during the Holidays. This is also great in an office setting or in a school classroom

Feel free to use the **30-day SAVERS** tracker to keep track of your consistency but also add anything else you'd like to stay consistent with at the bottom of the tracker.

If you'd like to reuse this item, make sure to laminate it so that you can use it again month after month.

If you are using The Miracle Morning as a family, make sure to use the **7-day CHARMS** Tracker. We suggest that you color it, laminate it, and use it daily with your children and/or in a classroom setting.

There's a **5-Page Activity Series** surrounding loyalty, excellence, passion, gratitude, and your vision for your future. These 5 part activity series is a perfect way to find out more about what lights up a child.

THE MIRACLE MORNING

A Note From Hal

Wherever you are in your life right now is both
temporary and exactly where you need to be in
order to experience what you need to experience
to become the person you need to be who is
capable of creating everything you want for your
life. So, be at peace with where you are while
maintaining a healthy sense of urgency to take
consistent action and make the progress each day
that will ensure you get to wherever it is
that you want to be.

I'm EXACTLY where I'm supposed to be to learn what I NEED to learn in order to BECOME the person I must be to CREATE the life I want.

www.miraclemorning.com

11

THE MIRACLE MORNING

A Note From Hal

Most people suffer from the self-limiting dysfunction I call the rear view mirror syndrome, driving through life with their subconscious mind constantly looking in their own self-limiting rear view mirror. They filter every choice they make through the limitations of their past experiences. Always remember that your potential is TRULY unlimited and that you are just as worthy, deserving, and capable of achieving everything you want as any other person on Earth.

I am blessed · I am focused · I am strong. I am hardworking · I am patient

I am wise ·

I am joyful ·

I am special · I am kind · I am

I believe
in my
potential
not in my past.

THE MIRACLE MORNING

A Note From Hal

Holding ourselves to the unattainable standard of perfection causes us to feel inadequate. When you realize that no one else expects you to be perfect, you can stop expecting it from yourself. Instead, strive every day to become the best version of yourself. Be okay with making mistakes, learn from them, and continue to get better. Be who you are. Love who you are. Others will too.

I GIVE UP BEING **PERFECT** FOR BEING **AUTHENTIC.**

-Hal Elrod

A Note From Hal

Now matters more than any other time in your life because it's what you are doing today that is determining who you're becoming, and who you're becoming will always determine the quality and direction of your life.

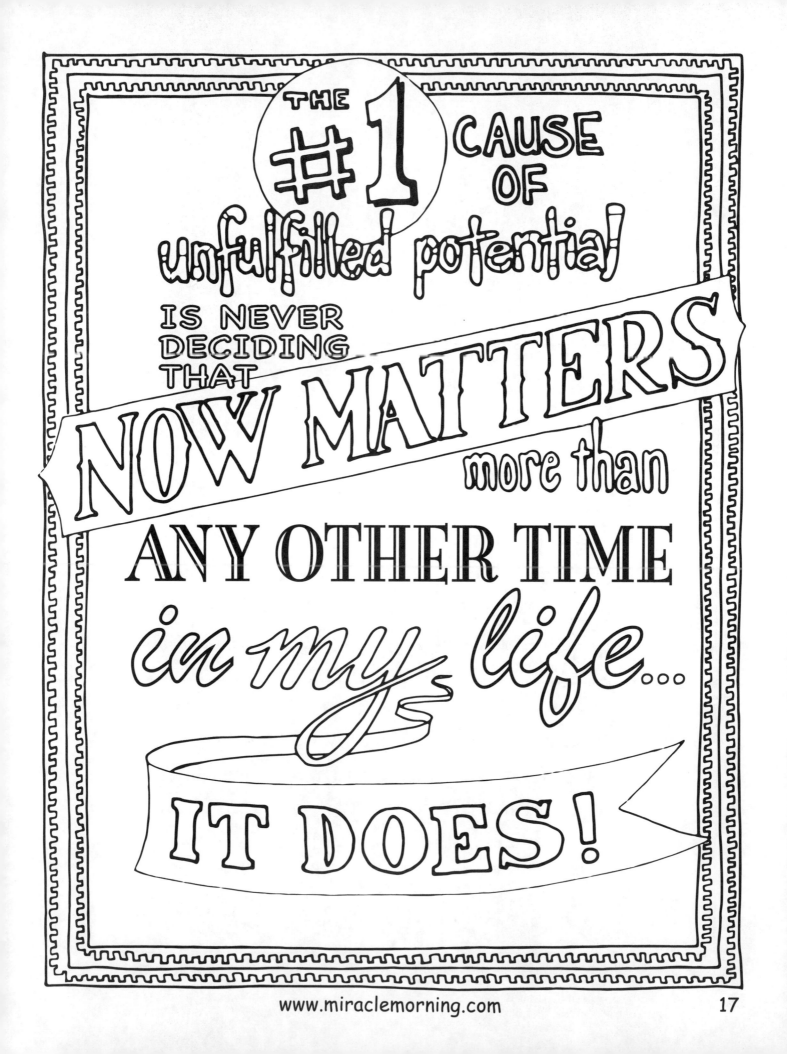

THE #1 CAUSE OF unfulfilled potential IS NEVER DECIDING THAT NOW MATTERS more than ANY OTHER TIME in my life... IT DOES!

A Note From Hal

You have unlimited potential because we have no limits other than those we place on ourselves. So, refuse to place self-imposed limitations on what's possible for your life. Think bigger than you've allowed yourself to think up until this point. Get clear on what you truly want, condition yourself to believe that it's possible by focusing on and affirming it every day, and then consistently move in the direction of your vision until it becomes your reality.

I am where I am because of who I was, but where I go depends entirely on who I choose to be.

HAL ELROD

THE MIRACLE MORNING

A Note From Hal

I think where people get caught up with accepting responsibility is when someone else is to blame for a situation. But understand that accepting responsibility is not the same as accepting blame. While blame determines who is at fault, responsibility determines who is committed to improving the circumstances. Don't worry about who is at fault; what matters is that YOU are committed to improving yourself and creating the circumstances you want for your life, regardless of who is to blame. That's the true power of accepting responsibility for everything in your life.

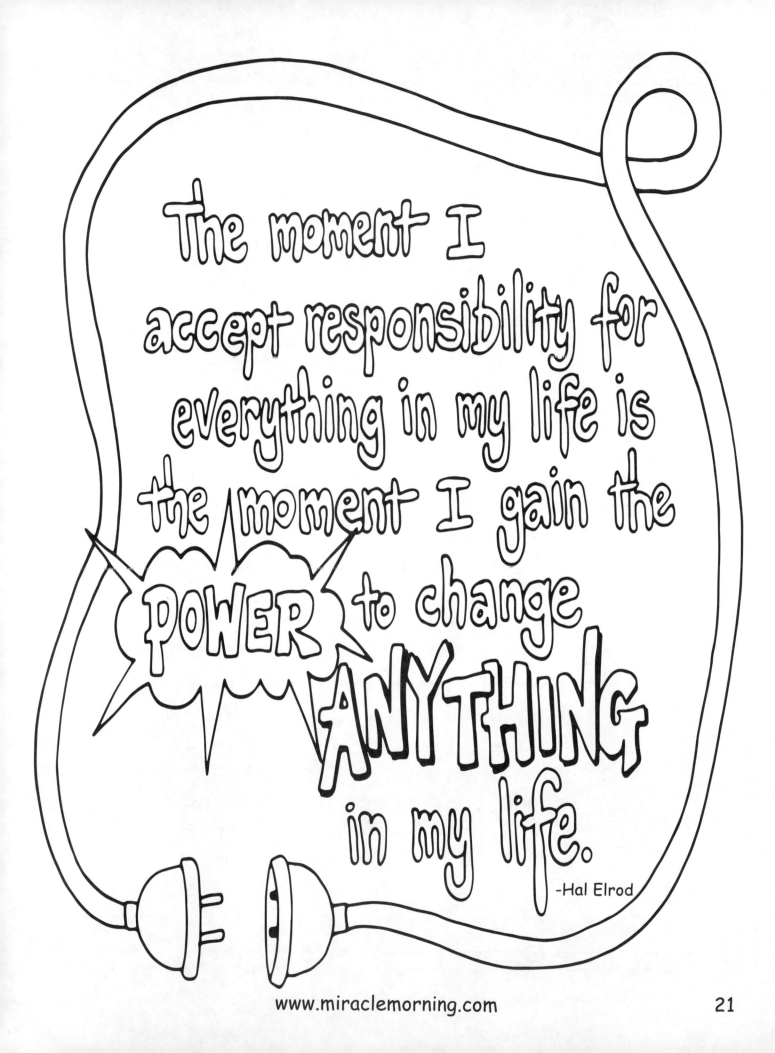

A Note From Hal

Happiness is a choice, and it's something that you choose from within. It's not hiding in a new car, dependent on another person, or some accomplishment that you're working towards. It is definitely not waiting to show up tomorrow. Happiness is available for you today—in every moment—and it has nothing to do with what's going on around you, and everything to do with what's going on inside of you. You experience happiness by accepting the things you can't change (such as your past), being grateful for all that you have, and actively creating progress, each day, toward all that you want.

I already have everything I need to be the HAPPIEST PERSON I can be; it's simply up to me to remember that in every moment.

-Hal Elrod

THE MIRACLE MORNING

A Note From Hal

In order to truly create the life of our dreams, we must first learn to love the life we have because the life you are living now is the same life you will be living in the future. Sure, the circumstances that you are going to create for yourself will undoubtedly be better than they are now, but it will still be your life, and it will be as good or bad as you choose to see it. If you aren't happy with what you've got now, then getting what you think you want isn't going to make you any happier. You must first love the life that you have unconditionally, while you are taking steps to create the life of your dreams.

I LOVE THE LIFE I HAVE WHILE I Create THE LIFE OF MY DREAMS. I DON'T HAVE TO CHOOSE ONE OVER THE OTHER.

A Note From Hal

Jim Rohn has been one of my greatest mentors and has taught me many life-changing philosophies. In my opinion, none was more life-changing than the concept that *our level of success (in any area of life) will rarely exceed our level of personal development (knowledge, skills, beliefs, habits, etc.) because our success is ultimately determined more by who we become.*

In other words, if you and I are measuring our levels of success in any area of our lives (finances, health, relationships, happiness, etc.) on a scale from one to ten, I think it's safe to say that we all want "Level 10" success, yes?

The not-so-obvious secret to that success is that we must invest time each day in our personal development, to cultivate the qualities and characteristics that will enable us to achieve and sustain the levels of success that we want. That is the purpose of *The Miracle Morning*.

My level of success will seldom exceed my level of personal development, because success is something I attract by the person I become. -Jim Rohn.

THE MIRACLE MORNING

A Note From Hal

Hundreds of thousands of individuals from around the world (most of whom had never before considered themselves to be a "morning person") have transformed their lives with *The Miracle Morning*, beginning with a commitment to do **The 30-Day Miracle Morning Life Transformation Challenge.**

You can download the free 30-Day Challenge at

for extra accountability.

By simply committing to wake up 30 minutes earlier than you usually would, and do the Life S.A.V.E.R.S. for just 30 days, you can make *The Miracle Morning* a part of your life, forever.

THE MIRACLE MORNING 30 DAY TRANSFORMATION TRACKER

	1	2	3	4	5	6	7	8	9	10	11	12	13	14	15	16	17	18	19	20	21	22	23	24	25	26	27	28	29	30
Silence																														
Affirmations																														
Visualization																														
Exercise																														
Reading																														
Scribing																														

THE MIRACLE MORNING

A Note From Hal

The essence of *The Miracle Morning* is
to simply begin each day by dedicating time
to the Life S.A.V.E.R.S. (Silence, Affirmations,
Visualization, Exercise, Reading, and Scribing)
so that you can become the person you need to
be to achieve the levels of health, wealth, love,
and success that you truly desire and deserve.
While most people go through life "wishing" and
"wanting" that they could have, be, and do so
much more, you are taking the necessary action
to ensure that you fulfill your potential and get
to create and live the most extraordinary
life you can imagine.

I dedicate TIME to the MIRACLE MORNING every day so that I CAN BECOME the Person I need to be to Create the LIFE I truly want & deserve

-Hal Elrod

A Note From Hal

Who we are becoming is far more important than what we're doing, and yet it's what we're doing each day that determines who we're becoming, which ultimately determines our quality of life and what we are capable of achieving. Every choice we make, big or small, contributes to the type of person we are becoming in terms of our mindset and our behavior. When the alarm clock goes off in the morning, how we respond sets the tone for who we are going to become that day. Either we hit the snooze button, thereby reinforcing a lack of self-discipline and the habit of procrastination. Or, we choose to wake up with discipline and purpose, thereby further developing the mindset and the behaviors that will enable us to continuously improve and reach the next level of our potential.

Who I become TODAY will determine what I am capable of creating TOMORROW.

-Hal Elrod

A Note From Hal

The Miracle Morning is made up of the six most powerful, effective, and time-tested personal development practices known to man ... now known as the Life S.A.V.E.R.S.

By combining the scientifically proven benefits of *Silence + Affirmations + Visualization + Exercise + Reading + Scribing* each morning, you will be starting each day with the ultimate morning ritual. You will quite literally be amongst the top .01% of our society who dedicates time everyday to their personal development.

You can customize the SAVERS to fit your lifestyle and use them daily to accelerate how quickly you're able to improve any area or achieve any results.

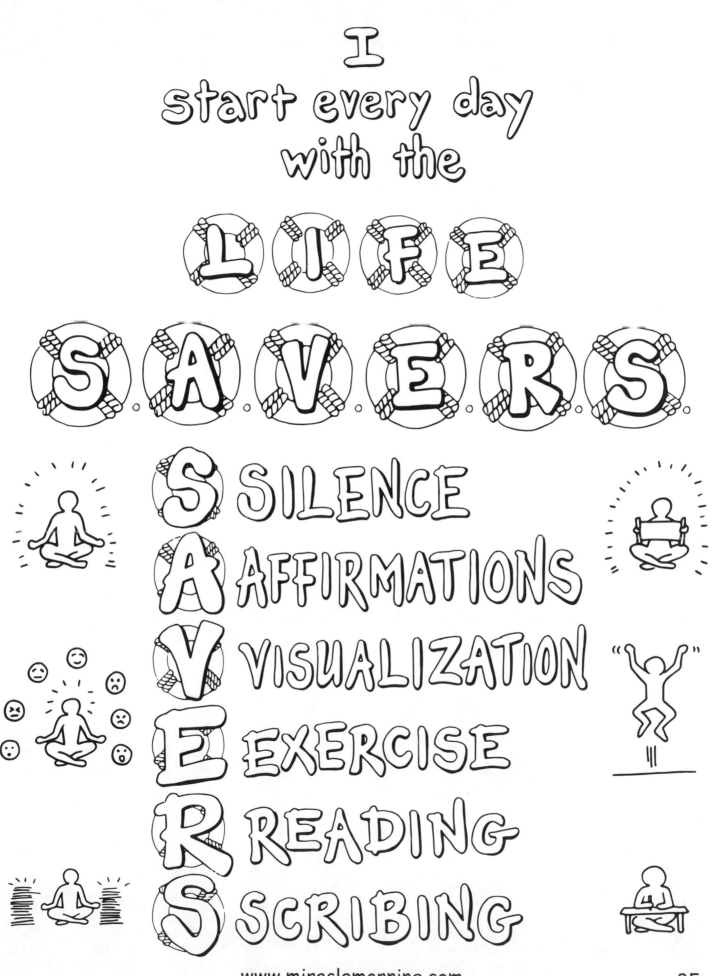

I
start every day
with the

LIFE
S.A.V.E.R.S.

S SILENCE
A AFFIRMATIONS
V VISUALIZATION
E EXERCISE
R READING
S SCRIBING

THE MIRACLE MORNING

A Note From Hal

For each of us to experience our best life, we must focus on making this year, and every year, the best year it can possibly be. Of course, to make this a great year, we must string together 365 of our best days, beginning with today. What is ONE thing you will commit to doing today, to ensure that you win the day, so that you can stay on track to make this your Best Year Yet?

A Note From Hal

If you could have, be, and do anything ...
what would you have, be, and do? Know that
you are just as worthy, deserving, and capable of
creating everything you want for your life as any
other person on Earth. Know that you are destined
for greatness, but you must choose it each day. You
must take the necessary actions each day (including
today) to move one step closer to creating, and
living, the life of your dreams.

What will you do today?

I AM Creating THE LIFE OF MY DREAMS

-Hal Elrod

A Note From Hal

Justin Ledford is living proof that vision boards work, as long as you're willing to put in the necessary work. Justin's dream of becoming an author, which had been on his vision board for many years, came true when he wrote and published his book, *Visions to the Top: A Millionaire's Secret Formula to Productivity, Visualization, and Meditation.*

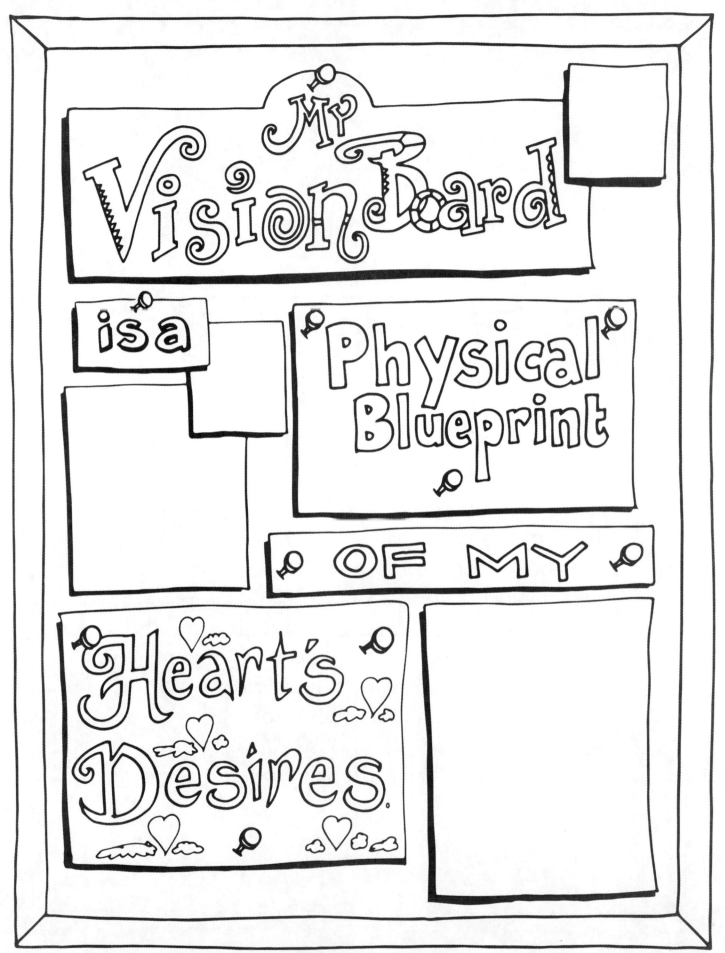

My Vision Board

is a

Physical Blueprint

OF MY

Heart's Desires.

THE MIRACLE MORNING

A Note From Hal

The Front Row Foundation is more than a cause, it is a metaphor and a movement about choosing to live every day to the fullest. While most people choose to be spectators, playing it safe and staying away from the action, we can choose to be participants in the Front Row of creating the life we want. As Jon Vroman, founder of the Front Row Foundation would say, "We don't always choose our seat, but we can always choose a Front Row experience." What life will you choose?
\o/

No matter what seat life gives me, I can ALWAYS choose to have a FRONT ROW Experience.

- Jon Vroman -

A Note From Hal

One of the most eye-opening realizations I've ever had that enabled me to overcome my excuses and start living to my full potential is that *how we live our lives gives other people permission to do the same.* This is especially true for the people closest to us, particularly our family, friends, and loved ones. I don't know about you, but that is a responsibility and power that I don't believe any of us should take lightly. If we settle for mediocrity in any area of our lives, we are (consciously or unconsciously) influencing those around us to do the same. For example, if we eat unhealthy foods and fail to exercise, the people we care about will feel that it's okay to eat unhealthy foods and skip exercise. However, when we wake up every day and take actions that are in alignment with living to our full potential, we inspire those around us to do the same.

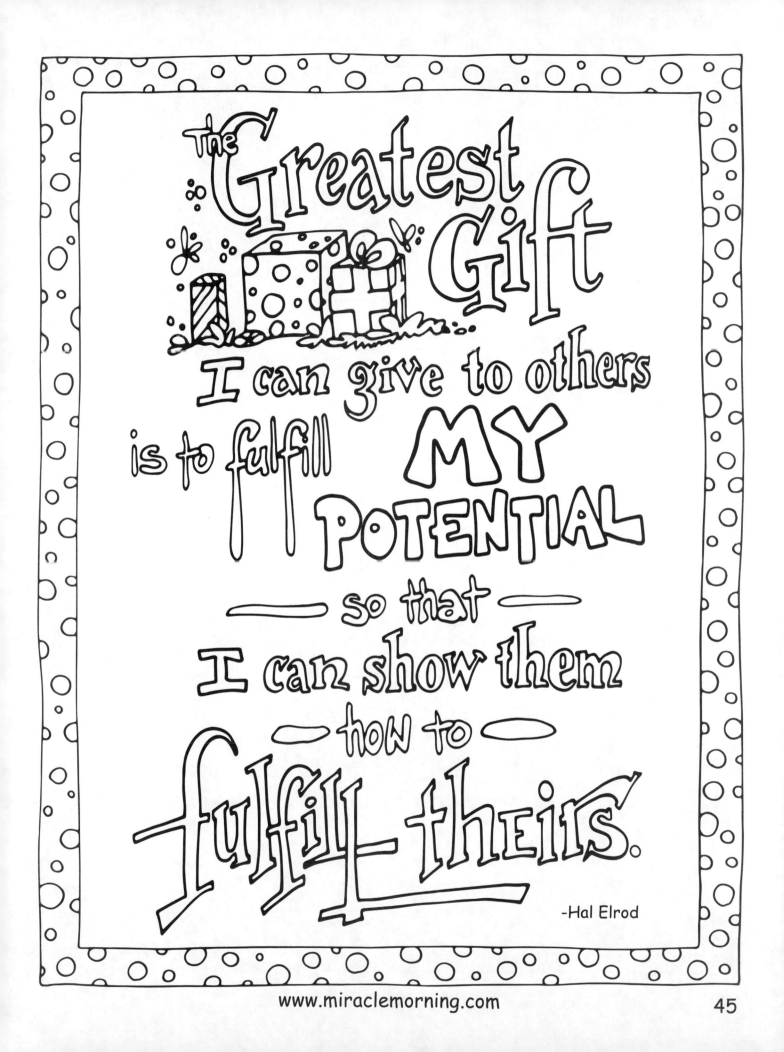

The Greatest Gift I can give to others is to fulfill MY POTENTIAL so that I can show them how to fulfill theirs.

-Hal Elrod

A Note From Hal

So often, we concern ourselves with what other people think of us and try hard to make the best impression. From what we wear when we get dressed in the morning, to what we post on social media, we say and do things in an attempt to "look good" to others. As Maya Angelou famously said, "I've learned that people will forget what you said, people will forget what you did, but people will never forget how you made them feel." People ultimately appreciate the value that you add to their lives much more than they care about what you wear or what kind of car you drive. In fact, the more value you add to a person's life, the more valuable you become to that person.

I DON'T WORRY ABOUT TRYING TO IMPRESS PEOPLE. Instead, I focus on how I can ADD VALUE TO THEIR LIVES.

-Hal Elrod

A Note From Hal

One significant factor that differentiates the world's most successful people from those who are settling for less than they truly want is their interpretation of, and response to, *fear*. Human nature is to allow our fears to dictate our actions. When we do this, it prevents us from taking the necessary steps towards what we're capable of, and deep down, what we truly want. As fellow human beings, even the most successful individuals have fears, but rather than allowing their fears to dictate their actions, they ensure that their *commitments* determine their actions. In other words, they do the things they're afraid of, despite their fears. And when they experience a setback, or fail to reach a goal, they learn from it, grow as a person, and focus on how they can be or do better next time.

There is nothing to fear because I cannot fail. Only LEARN, GROW, and become BETTER than I've ever been before.

THE MIRACLE MORNING

A Note From Hal

Research has proven that gratitude and happiness go hand in hand. The people who invest time each day focusing on what they're grateful for are, on average, 40 percent happier than those who don't. The amount, or rather, *depth* of gratitude that we are present to, largely determines how we feel about our lives. When you are consciously aware of all that you have to be grateful for, you give yourself permission to feel good about all that you have, rather than an excuse to feel bad about what you don't. The more gratitude that we actively cultivate each day, and express to others, the happier and more fulfilled we will be.

EXPERIENCE G.R.A.T.I.T.U.D.E. AT A DEEPER LEVEL:

Give it...

Receive it...

Affirm it...

Think about what I'm grateful for...

Inspire gratitude in others...

Talk about what I'm grateful for...

Understand how important gratitude is...

Dream about what I'm grateful for...

Express gratitude today and every day...

-Hal Elrod

THE MIRACLE MORNING

A Note From Hal

One of the most important beliefs to reinforce through your affirmations is that you always have limitless potential to change or improve any aspect of your life. You are just as worthy, deserving, and capable of creating and achieving everything you desire as any other person on Earth. You must first embrace that truth and then align your (daily) actions to transform your desires into your reality. It doesn't matter what you have or haven't done up until this point because you can give up who you've been for who you choose to become. While you can't go back in time and change the past, you can change everything else, starting now.

I have the ability to CHANGE or Create anything in my life, starting now.

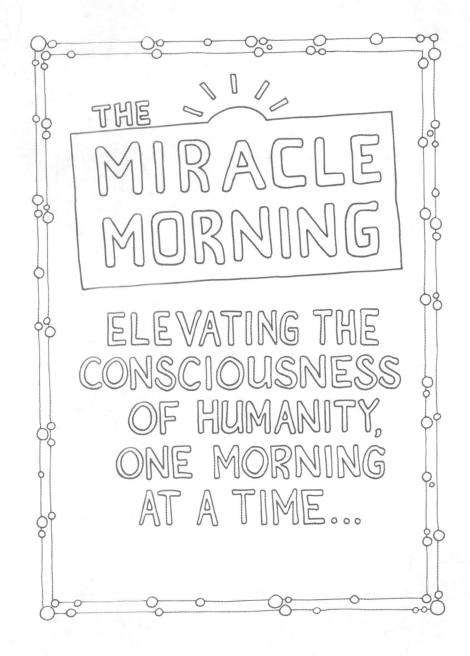

I'm EXACTLY where I'm supposed to be to learn what I NEED to learn in order to BECOME the person I must be to CREATE the life I want.

I believe in my potential not in my past.

I am focused · I am strong · I am hardworking · I am patient · I am kind · I am special · I am joyful · I am wise · I am blessed ·

I GIVE UP BEING PERFECT FOR BEING AUTHENTIC.

THE

MIRACLE MORNING

ELEVATING THE CONSCIOUSNESS OF HUMANITY, ONE MORNING AT A TIME...

THE #1 CAUSE OF unfulfilled potential IS NEVER DECIDING THAT NOW MATTERS more than ANY OTHER TIME in my life... IT DOES!

I am where I am because of who I was, but where I go depends entirely on who I choose to be.

The moment I accept responsibility for everything in my life is the moment I gain the POWER to change ANYTHING in my life.

THE MIRACLE MORNING

ELEVATING THE CONSCIOUSNESS OF HUMANITY, ONE MORNING AT A TIME...

My level of success will seldom exceed my level of personal development, because success is something I attract by the person I become.

I LOVE THE LIFE I HAVE WHILE I Create THE LIFE OF MY DREAMS. I DON'T HAVE TO CHOOSE ONE OVER THE OTHER.

I already have everything I need to be the HAPPIEST PERSON I can be; it's simply up to me to remember that in every moment.

THE **MIRACLE MORNING**

ELEVATING THE CONSCIOUSNESS OF HUMANITY, ONE MORNING AT A TIME...

I
start every day
with the

L I F E
S.A.V.E.R.S.

S SILENCE
A AFFIRMATIONS
V VISUALIZATION
E EXERCISE
R READING
S SCRIBING

THE **MIRACLE** **30** **DAY**
MORNING
TRANSFORMATION TRACKER

	1	2	3	4	5	6	7	8	9	10	11	12	13	14	15	16	17	18	19	20	21	22	23	24	25	26	27	28	29	30
SILENCE																														
AFFIRMATIONS																														
VISUALIZATION																														
EXERCISE																														
READING																														
SCRIBING																														

Who I become
TODAY
will determine what I am
capable of creating
TOMORROW.

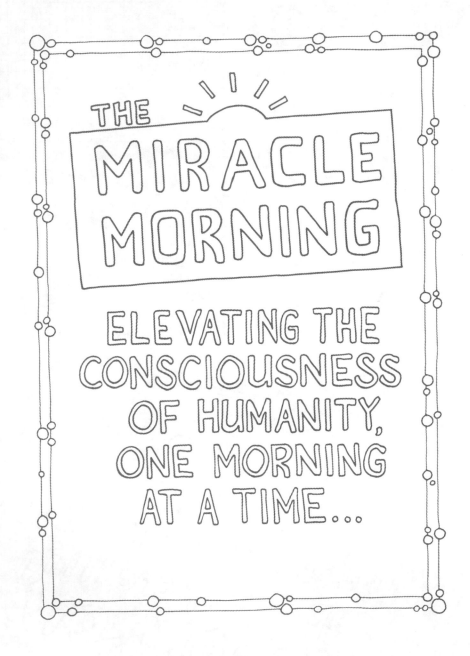

I dedicate TIME to the MIRACLE MORNING every day so that I CAN BECOME the person I need to be to Create the LIFE I truly want & deserve

JAN
FEB
MAR
APR
MAY
JUN
JUL
AUG
SEPT
OCT
NOV
DEC

I am ready & committed to make THIS my BEST year YET

My Vision Board is a "Physical" Blueprint OF MY Heart's Desires.

I DON'T WORRY ABOUT TRYING TO IMPRESS PEOPLE. Instead, I focus on how I can ADD VALUE TO THEIR LIVES.

No matter what seat life gives me, I can ALWAYS choose to have a FRONT ROW Experience.

The Greatest Gift I can give to others is to fulfill MY POTENTIAL — so that — I can show them how to fulfill theirs.

I AM CREATING THE LIFE OF MY DREAMS.

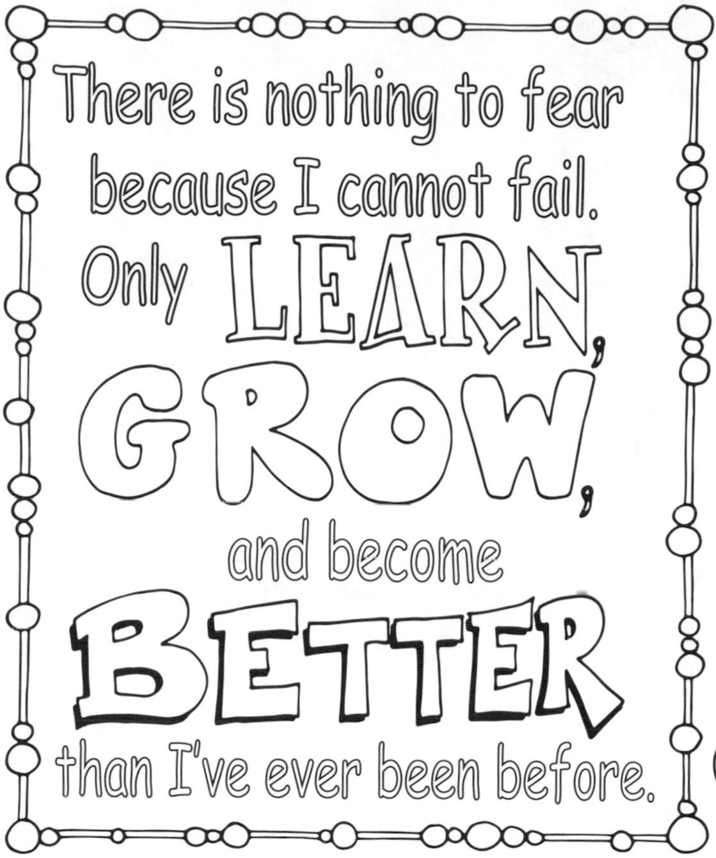

There is nothing to fear because I cannot fail. Only **LEARN**, **GROW**, and become **BETTER** than I've ever been before.

I have the ability to **CHANGE** or **Create** anything in my life, starting now.

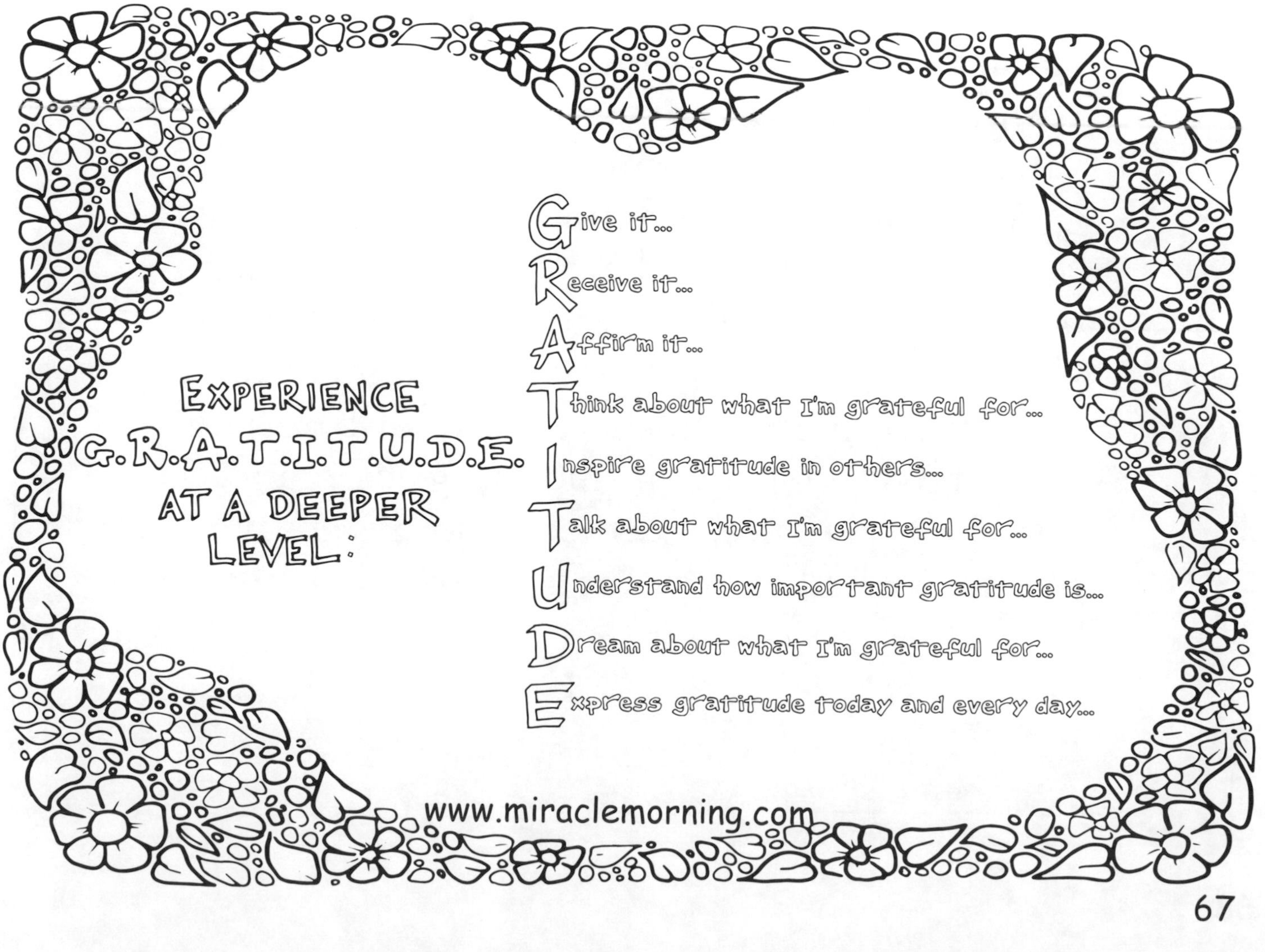

EXPERIENCE G.R.A.T.I.T.U.D.E. AT A DEEPER LEVEL:

Give it...
Receive it...
Affirm it...
Think about what I'm grateful for...
Inspire gratitude in others...
Talk about what I'm grateful for...
Understand how important gratitude is...
Dream about what I'm grateful for...
Express gratitude today and every day...

www.miraclemorning.com

THE MIRACLE MORNING

Mindfulness Tip from Julianna Raye

Kids learn by example, so the care and attention you give to anything you've chosen to do teaches them. As you sit coloring together with your child or on your own, let coloring be the most important thing in the world. Give your wholehearted attention to it. Kids do this naturally, so they can be your teacher. Notice details about the process of coloring, the colors, the forms, the desire to stay in the lines or not. Bring an appreciation and sense of discovery to the activity of coloring and bring acceptance to the experience, whether or not it's always pleasant, whether or not it goes just as planned.

Mindfulness Tip from Julianna Raye

Try focusing just on the sights associated with coloring today, *see*. This is an eyes open meditation. Pay attention to what you see as you color and let what you hear or feel be in the background of your attention. So, if a sound or feeling pulls your focus, gently bring your attention back to what you're seeing. If you'd like, you can say the label see out loud or to yourself every few seconds to keep you on track. As you fill in the shapes with color, constant change is happening. Black and white shapes are transforming before your eyes with each shift of your marker or crayon. Track that change with your attention——go along for the ride your marker goes on as you fill in the shapes with color. You can notice each transition as well——reaching for and choosing a different color and bringing the new marker back to the paper. Track that visually. Paying attention to everything you see as you color will develop the skills of concentration power, sensory clarity, and equanimity.

Mindfulness Tip from Julianna Raye

Today let's focus only on *hear*. This may be tricky since coloring is a very visual activity but just give it a try. Think of it as a game and we're upping the ante— you don't have to play well, you just have to play at all! Pay attention to what you hear as you color and let what you see or feel be in the background. When *see* or *feel* pull your focus, gently bring your attention back to *hear*. If you'd like, you can use the label *hear* out loud or to yourself every few seconds, to keep you on track. Some examples of *hear* might be the silence in the room, the sound of the marker or crayon against the paper, the creak of your chair, any noise in the background or any self-talk in your mind. Usually noises or self-talk would feel like a distraction, but in this case they're helping you develop the essential skills of concentration, clarity, and equanimity. If your attention is split and you're noticing both *see* and *hear*, that's no problem. Just try to emphasize *hear*—that's where the workout is.

Mindfulness Tip from Julianna Raye

Guess what we're focusing on today? You got it, *feel*. Notice physical or emotional sensations as you color today. You might feel interested or entertained as you color. If so, where is that feeling of interest or entertainment located in the body? How strong is it? Does it come and go? If you're sitting with your child, you might have spontaneous loving feelings toward them. You can choose to notice that and by giving your caring attention to the experience, you grow it. You might also choose to focus on the physical sensation—the feeling of the marker in your hand or the way your body feels as you sit and color. You can say that label *feel* every few seconds to keep yourself on track. And when *see* or *hear* pull your focus, gently bring your attention back to *feel*.

Mindfulness Tip from Julianna Raye

Today as you color, try allowing your attention to move freely between *see*, *hear*, and *feel*, labeling what you notice accordingly. You don't need to label every experience you notice. Find a pace that's comfortable for you and take a few seconds with each experience you're labeling. For example, you may notice the shape you're coloring *see* then your chair creaking *hear* then the silence in the room *hear* then the way the marker feels in your hand feel. It's ok if you notice the same experience more than once, it's ok to be late with your label, and it's ok to guess. If you notice more than one category, just pick one to focus on. If you get on a roll and your concentration is high, you can also feel free to drop the labels and continue staying with each experience you notice for a few seconds at a time. If an experience disappears as you notice it——no problem——just pick something new to focus on and label.

Mindfulness Tip from Julianna Raye

Parents often wonder how they can help their kids meditate. As you get more skillful, you'll naturally find opportunities to show them what you've learned. One powerful way to start is to notice how you relate to your child's emotions. In the same way that you're becoming curious, interested, and accepting of your own emotional life, whether the emotion is pleasant or unpleasant, you can do the same with your child. When you're able to greet your child's unpleasant emotions with focus, clarity, and acceptance and when you're able to notice and process what emotions may be triggered in you as a reaction, you break that cycle of reactivity, and you prevent things from escalating. Likewise, when you're fully present (in other words, concentrated, clear, and equanimous) as your child is expressing a positive emotion, you have a richer experience of the moment, which fosters a deeper connection with your child.

THE MIRACLE MORNING

Mindfulness activity: Kindness for all

Think of something kind
you wish for someone you care about…

Now, think of something kind
you wish for yourself…

Can you think of something kind
you wish for someone you don't even know?

Lastly, think of one kind wish
for someone who you're not a big fan of.

Can you notice how these kind
wishes shift how you feel right now?

THE MIRACLE MORNING

A Note from Mike & Lindsay McCarthy
co-authors of The Miracle Morning for Parents & Families

After about a month of doing Life S.A.V.E.R.S., our son, Tyler, was having a hard time connecting with the acronym. So, as Hal suggests in *The Miracle Morning*, we customized the acronym to fit Tyler's needs. Tyler and I got out a piece of scrap paper and wrote out all the words in Life S.A.V.E.R.S. then started playing with them.

Since our daughter, Ember, didn't know her letters yet, we had been using creativity in place of Scribing. So, we started there: "C" for creativity. Affirmations in our opinion couldn't be changed, so we kept "A" for affirmations.

Like most kids, ours have a hard time with silence, and most of their visualization was done through guided meditations. So we decided to combine silence and visualization into one category called meditation: "M" for meditation. We expanded the exercise to include a healthy breakfast. So we renamed it "H" for health. We wanted to keep it at six letters, so we added an "S" for service because it is something important to us that we wanted to instill in our children.

After unscrambling the letters, we came up with C.H.A.R.M.S. Tyler was so happy with the new acronym. He had helped to create his own Miracle Morning routine, and he couldn't wait to get started! Involving the kids in their own Miracle Morning so that they could have a morning ritual too was bringing our family closer together.

If you try this practice with your children, remember to be flexible and forgiving with yourself and them. It's not about perfection. It's about priming your kids so they will want to do it on their own. We do not wake our kids up early to do their Miracle Morning, but have them do it once they wake on their own. If your children are older, they can make the choice to wake up early to complete their C.H.A.R.M.S., but I wouldn't force them to do it. Our kids always have the choice to do them or not, but they are not allowed any "screen time" (TV, iPad, etc.) until all six are completed. Some days it takes them all day to complete their Miracle Morning!

	S	M	T	W	Th	F	S
C Creativity	☐	☐	☐	☐	☐	☐	☐
H Health	☐	☐	☐	☐	☐	☐	☐
A Affirmation	☐	☐	☐	☐	☐	☐	☐
R Reading	☐	☐	☐	☐	☐	☐	☐
M Meditation	☐	☐	☐	☐	☐	☐	☐
S Service	☐	☐	☐	☐	☐	☐	☐

THE
MIRACLE
MORNING

ELEVATING THE
CONSCIOUSNESS
OF HUMANITY,
ONE MORNING
AT A TIME...

THE MIRACLE MORNING

ELEVATING THE CONSCIOUSNESS OF HUMANITY, ONE MORNING AT A TIME...

PEOPLE · LOVE · BEING · AROUND · ME

THE **MIRACLE MORNING**

ELEVATING THE CONSCIOUSNESS OF HUMANITY, ONE MORNING AT A TIME...

EVERYTHING IS RIGHT ABOUT YOU

DR JILL KAHN

I WILL cheerfully GIVE PEOPLE MORE THAN THEY EXPECT

THE MIRACLE MORNING

ELEVATING THE CONSCIOUSNESS OF HUMANITY, ONE MORNING AT A TIME...

I stand up for what is important to me.

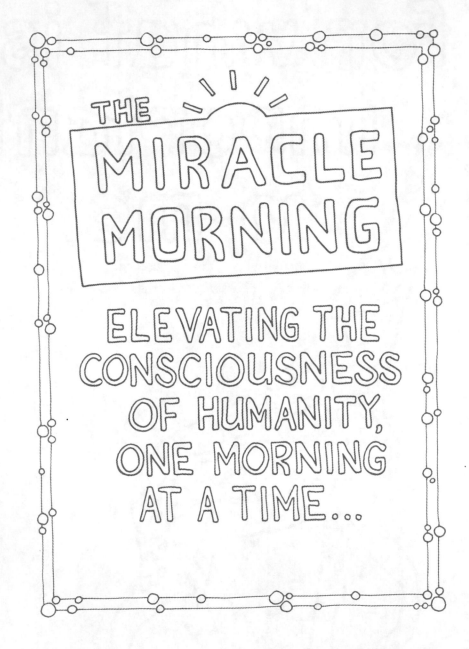

I AM **POWERFUL** BEYOND MEASURE

I AM **STRONGER** THAN I THINK

I AM **BRAVER** THAN I SEEM

I AM **BLESSED** WITH ALL I NEED

– PATRICIA MORENO –

I am Confident.
I am GROWING.
I am HONEST.
I am loved.
I am Unique.
I am reliable.
I am fuzzy.
I am Brave.
I am inspirational.

THE

MIRACLE MORNING

ELEVATING THE CONSCIOUSNESS OF HUMANITY, ONE MORNING AT A TIME...

When I FOCUS on what's GREAT in my life, more of what's GREAT will magically appear.

I am STRONG

I can DO HARD THiNGS

THE MIRACLE MORNING

ELEVATING THE CONSCIOUSNESS OF HUMANITY, ONE MORNING AT A TIME...

THE MIRACLE MORNING

ELEVATING THE CONSCIOUSNESS OF HUMANITY, ONE MORNING AT A TIME...

THE MIRACLE MORNING

ELEVATING THE CONSCIOUSNESS OF HUMANITY, ONE MORNING AT A TIME...

Who are the most loyal people in your life?
Color a card and give it to them to let them know!

THE

MIRACLE MORNING

ELEVATING THE CONSCIOUSNESS OF HUMANITY, ONE MORNING AT A TIME...

What are you excellent at?
Write it down and put it somewhere it will remind you every day!

I am
Passionate about...

I am
Passionate about...

I am Passionate.

What are you passionate about?
Write it down, cut it out, and share it with someone you want to inspire!

I am
Passionate about...

I am
Passionate about...

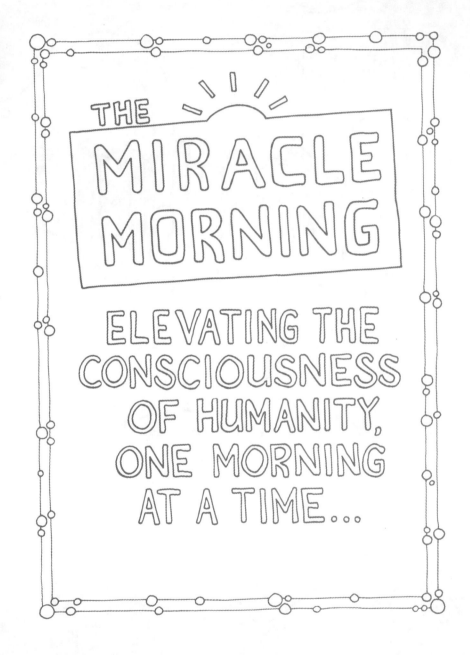

THE

MIRACLE
MORNING

ELEVATING THE
CONSCIOUSNESS
OF HUMANITY,
ONE MORNING
AT A TIME...

My Vision Board

What will your vision board look like?

THE MIRACLE MORNING

ELEVATING THE CONSCIOUSNESS OF HUMANITY, ONE MORNING AT A TIME...

PEOPLE · LOVE · BEING · AROUND · ME

EVERYTHING IS RIGHT ABOUT YOU

DR JILL KAHN

I will cheerfully give people more than they expect

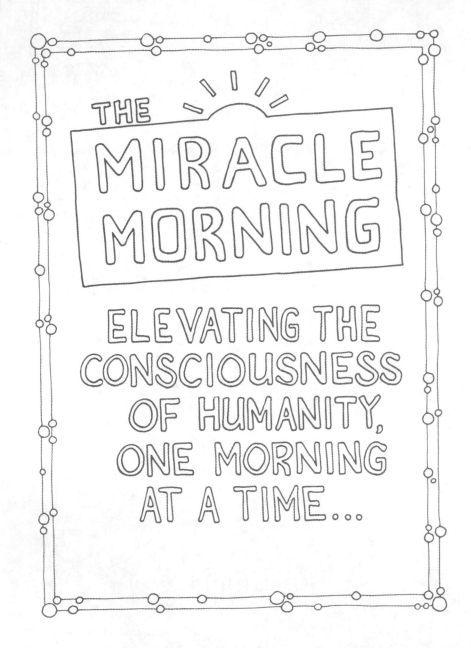

THE MIRACLE MORNING

ELEVATING THE CONSCIOUSNESS OF HUMANITY, ONE MORNING AT A TIME...

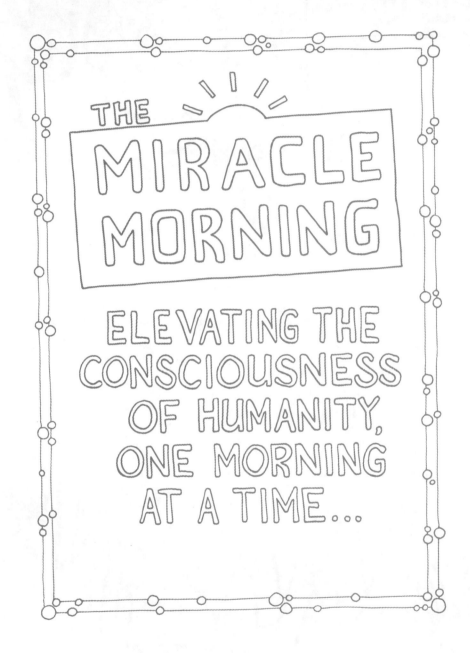

I AM LOYAL.

I am Excellent.

I stand up for what is important to me.

THE MIRACLE MORNING

ELEVATING THE CONSCIOUSNESS OF HUMANITY, ONE MORNING AT A TIME...

When I FOCUS on what's GREAT in my life, more of what's GREAT will magically appear.

I am CONFIDENT.
I am GROWING.
I am HONEST.
I am loved.
I am Unique.
I am reliable.
I am funny.
I am Brave.
I am inspirational.

I AM GRATEFUL FOR

I AM GRATEFUL FOR

What am I Grateful for? Everything

I AM GRATEFUL FOR

I AM GRATEFUL FOR

THE **MIRACLE MORNING**

ELEVATING THE CONSCIOUSNESS OF HUMANITY, ONE MORNING AT A TIME...

I am STRONG

I can Do HARD THINGS

I AM POWERFUL BEYOND MEASURE

I AM STRONGER THAN I THINK

I AM BRAVER THAN I SEEM

I AM BLESSED WITH ALL I NEED

— PATRICIA MORENO —

Use this space to write or draw your own affirmations

THE **MIRACLE MORNING**

ELEVATING THE CONSCIOUSNESS OF HUMANITY, ONE MORNING AT A TIME...

138

One of Hal's Favorite Affirmation Formulas...

I am just as worthy, deserving, and capable of

_____

_____

(whatever you deeply want, but are holding yourself back from)

as any other person on Earth, and I will prove that by doing

_____

_____

(the specific action[s] that will move you forward) today.

— A SPECIAL INVITATION — FROM HAL

Fans and readers of *The Miracle Morning* make up an extraordinary community of like-minded individuals who wake up each day dedicated to fulfilling the unlimited potential that is within all of us. As the author of *The Miracle Morning*, it was my desire to create an online space where readers and fans could go to connect, get encouragement, share best practices, support one another, discuss the book, post videos, find an accountability partner, and even swap smoothie recipes and exercise routines.

I honestly had no idea that The Miracle Morning Community would become one of the most inspiring, engaged, and supportive online communities in the world, but it has. I'm blown away by the caliber of our 350,000+ members, which consists of people from all around the globe and is growing daily.

Just go to www.MyTMMCommunity.com and request to join The Miracle Morning Community (on Facebook). Here you'll be able to connect with others who are already practicing The Miracle Morning—many of whom have been doing it for years—to get additional support and accelerate your success.

I'll be moderating the community and checking in regularly. I look forward to seeing you there!

If you'd like to connect with me personally on social media, follow **@HalElrod** on Twitter and **Facebook.com/YoPalHal** on Facebook. Please feel free to send me a direct message, leave a comment, or ask me a question. I do my best to answer every single one, so let's connect soon!

— ABOUT THE AUTHORS —

HAL ELROD is one of the highest rated keynote speakers in America, but is best known as the author of what is now being widely regarded as "one of the most life-changing books ever written" (and is quickly becoming one of the highest rated books on Amazon, with over 1,500 five-star reviews), *The Miracle Morning: The Not-So-Obvious Secret Guaranteed To Transform Your Life … (Before 8AM)*. Hal died at age 20. Hit head-on by a drunk driver at 70 miles per hour, he broke 11 bones, was clinically dead for six minutes, spent six days in a coma, and was told he would never walk again. Defying the logic of doctors and the temptations to be a victim, Hal went on to not only walk but to run a 52-mile ultramarathon, become a hall of fame business achiever, an international keynote speaker, host of one of the top success podcasts on iTunes called *Achieve Your Goals with Hal Elrod*, and most importantly … he is grateful to be alive and living the life of his dreams with his wife, Ursula, and their two children, Sophie and Halsten. For more information on Hal's speaking, writing, and coaching, please visit **HalElrod.com**

BRIANNA GREENSPAN is the founder of Brianna Greenspan International, an educational consulting firm helping adults and children throughout the world. She is an author, educator, coach and consultant in the leadership development and wellness field inspiring millions to live to their full potential. Brianna is on a mission to develop products and services to elevate humanity. She has been trained in Xchange facilitation as well as the Unified Mindfulness approach and uses both methodologies within all her workshops, trainings and coaching.

Brianna has been in the personal development field for over 14 years which started by her overcoming her own genetic physical challenges. Her unwavering devotion for healthy living, personal development, coupled with her passion for the Miracle Morning movement and Everything Is Right About You movement made for a perfect opportunity to impact and lead school communities in sharing practices to enable success. **Learn more at: BriannaGreenspan.com**

PAUL JOY has been part of the Miracle Morning movement for years. He enjoys the quiet of early mornings, rising hours before his wife and three children to explore S.A.V.E.R.S. and begin each day on his terms. He credits the Miracle Morning for bringing structure and purpose into his morning routine. This has helped fill his own cup, daily, and be equipped to encourage and uphold others. Paul is a teacher and school chaplain in Melbourne, Australia where he shares lessons and stories with students and the wider school community. He is an inspiring speaker who intrigues his audience with creative and fun styles of presentation and engagement.

Paul received his first Calligraphy set at age 10 and has been playing with handmade lettering and scripts in his spare time ever since. He enjoys making sketchnotes to help illustrate ideas and messages at workshops and conferences, both in-person and online. He creates inspiring hand-drawn card designs for customers on a monthly subscription to help keep the art of handwritten cards and personal notes alive. His illustrations feature in several non-fiction publications and he's just finished illustrating his first picture-story book.

Holding firm to the belief that JOY is available and accessible to everyone, Paul is a strong advocate for making time to restore and refresh oneself. Creativity, coloring and words of affirmation are important ingredients in his endeavors to be a positive influence in the lives of all who encounter him and his work. Find out more at **BrushWithJoy.com** and follow Paul on Instagram @brushwithjoy

HONORÉE CORDER is the author of 20 books, including You Must Write a Book, Vision to Reality, Prosperity for Writers, Business Dating, The Successful Single Mom Book Series, If Divorce is a Game, and The Divorced Phoenix. She is also Hal Elrod's business partner in The Miracle Morning Book Series. She coaches business professionals, writers, and aspiring non-fiction authors who want to publish their books to bestseller status, create a platform, and develop multiple streams of income. **Learn more at HonoreeCorder.com.**

BOOK BRIANNA TO SPEAK!

ONLINE SPEAKING & PROFESSIONAL DEVELOPMENT SESSIONS

Brianna is an executive leadership coach for principals and administrations in the academic space as well as executive leadership teams who are looking for support with resilience, mindset, and utilizing The Miracle Morning in a collaborative and team setting to increase productivity and overall well-being in the workplace.

Brianna was exceptional. She delivered a framework to my client that has enhanced their focus and productivity. They still talk about her segment months after our event.

– Michael OBrien
Peloton Executive Coaching & Pause Breathe Reflect Sangha

BOOK HAL TO SPEAK!

Book Hal As Your Keynote Speaker and You're Guaranteed to Make Your Event Highly Enjoyable & Unforgettable!

For more than a decade, Hal Elrod has been consistently rated as the #1 Keynote Speaker by meeting planners and attendees. His unique style combines inspiring audiences with his unbelieveable TRUE story, keeping them laughing hysterically with his high energy, stand-up comedy style delivery, and empowering them with actionable strategies to take their RESULTS to the next level.

"Hal received a 9.8 out of 10 from our members. That never happens."
– Entrepreneur Organization (NYC Chapter)

"Hal was the featured keynote speaker for 400 of our top sales performers and executive team. He gave us a plan that was so simple, we had no choice but to put it into action immediately."
– Art Van Furniture

"Bringing Hal in to be the keynote speaker at our annual conference was the best investment we could have made."
– Fidelity National Title

For More Info - Visit www.HalElrod.com

THE MIRACLE MORNING SERIES

The Journal

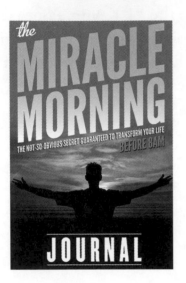

For Network Marketers

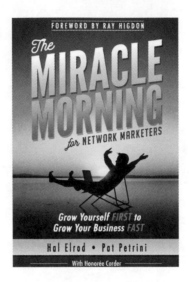

For Real Estate Agents

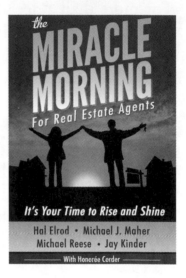

For Salespeople

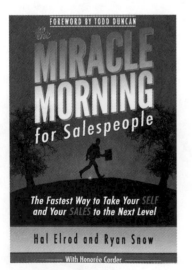

For Writers

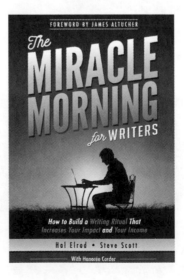

For College Students

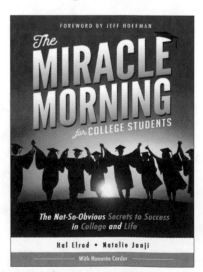

For Teachers

For Network Marketers

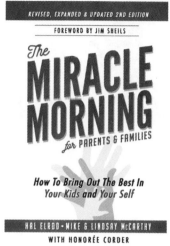

For Millionaires

For Couples

For Addiction Recovery

For Entrepreneurs

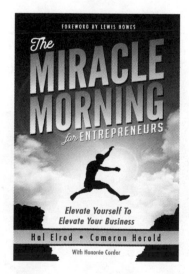

COMING SOON...

The Miracle Morning for Seniors Coming Soon

THE MIRACLE MORNING SERIES

COMPANION GUIDES & WORKBOOKS

Art of
Affirmations

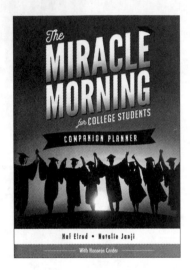

Companion
Planner

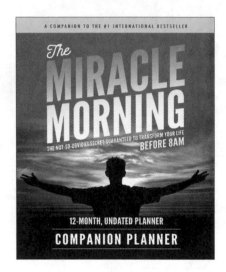

for Network Marketers
90-Day Action PlanGuide

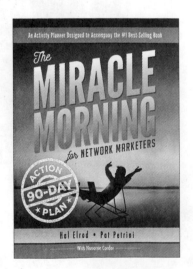

for Salespeople
Companion Guide

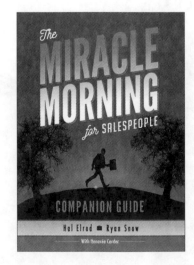